Brantwood, photographed from the air on 23 August 1947

BRANTWOOD

The story of John Ruskin's Coniston home

James S. Dearden

Master of the Guild of St George

The Ruskin Foundation

2009

First published as *A Short History of Brantwood* in 1967;
second edition, 1974

Revised edition
© Text, James S. Dearden 2009

ISBN 978-0-9550938-3-8

The Ruskin Foundation
Brantwood, Coniston, Cumbria LA21 8AD

Keystones to the Brantwood arches, commissioned by The Ruskin Association in 1975

Typeset & Design by Desktop Studio, Bembridge, PO35 5US
Printed by Berforts Information Press Ltd.

Preface

I have known Brantwood for more than sixty years. I have known and liked Brantwood for longer than J. Howard Whitehouse, who in 1932 had the opportunity of buying the house and establishing it as an international memorial to that great Victorian, John Ruskin.

In 1937 Whitehouse published his *Ruskin and Brantwood. An account of the Exhibition Rooms.* On 22 August 1947 I visited him at Brantwood and he gave me a copy of his book, inscribing it for me "In memory of a happy day at Brantwood. 22 August 1947. J. Howard Whitehouse." On the following day the aerial photograph of Brantwood, reproduced as the frontispiece to this book, was taken. Whitehouse is the tiny figure standing on the balcony, looking at the aircraft.

The first edition of my *Short History of Brantwood* was published in 1967 as a student project by Twickenham College of Technology, an organisation which was then associated with Brantwood; they re-printed the book in 1974. One of my copies of this book is so filled with manuscript revisions, corrections and additions that it seemed to be high time for a new revised and expanded edition, and I am grateful to The Ruskin Foundation for publishing it.

In the preparation of this new edition I have been helped by many friends. Sir Christopher Audland has added to my knowledge of the Hudsons and their circle. Howard Hull has kindly taken many photographs at Brantwood and the Ruskin Museum, Coniston, for me. In the Ruskin Library at Lancaster University, Rebecca Patterson, Diane Tyler and Jan Shepherd have been unfailingly kind and helpful and I am very grateful to them. Paul Dawson has generously allowed me to use his photographs of the Brantwood arches keystones. I am indebted to architect Jack Thompson for his drawing of the original Brantwood Cottage and to Becky Samuelson for her artistic expertise. I am obliged to English Heritage for allowing me to use the aerial photograph of Brantwood, to The Ruskin Museum, Coniston, for the use of the Rock Harmonicon image, and to the National Archives Image Library for the photograph by T. A. & J. Green

J.S.D.

20 January 2009

Arthur Severn's 1892 view of Coniston Old Man from Brantwood captures Father West's description of a century earlier

BRANTWOOD

1 *Brantwood's early days*

The eighteenth century writers of guide books to the Lake District owe much to Father Thomas West. West's *Guide*, originally published in 1778, was not the first, but was certainly one of the most popular of the early books.

To facilitate his description of the scenery, West established a number of "stations" or points from which the best views could be seen to advantage. One of his stations was on the east side of Coniston Lake, near the point where Beck Leven enters the lake, a short distance south of Brantwood. He also extolled the virtues of a view to be had

> in the boat, and from the centre of the lake, opposite to Coniston-hall. Looking towards the mountains, the lake spreads itself into a noble expanse of transparent water, and bursts into a bay on each side, bordered with verdant meadows, and inclosed with a variety of grounds rising in an exceedingly bold manner. The objects are beautifully diversified amongst themselves, and contrasted by the finest exhibition of rural elegance (cultivation and pasturage, waving woods, and sloping inclosures, adorned by nature and improved by art) under the bold sides of stupendous mountains, whose airy summits the elevated eye cannot now reach, and which almost deny access to the human kind.

About 1797 Thomas Woodville bought a three acre plot of steep, rocky and wooded land near to West's "station" from the Gaskarth family who had Coniston Hall and who owned land in Monk Coniston. On it Woodville built a small house to command the view across the lake. The property was called "Brantwood Cottage" (from *brant*, a local word for *steep*).

The house had four rooms on the ground floor – the hall, the two rooms which now form the study and part of what is now the shop area – together with the rooms above.

In 1818 Woodville subscribed £15 towards the building of the new parish church, and in the following year he bought a house called Yewdale Grove, at Yewdale Bridge on the edge of Coniston, from Sir Daniel le Fleming. He continued to own Brantwood until 1823 when he sold the house to Samuel Carrington. Carrington owned Brantwood until 1827 but seems to have done little or nothing to make his stay noteworthy.

An architect's impression of the original 18th century Brantwood Cottage

The next owners of Brantwood were Edward and Anne Copley of Thorp Arch, Doncaster. Three years later Anne Copley died here, bequeathing the house to her daughter, who was also called Anne.

This second Anne Copley began to enlarge Brantwood. In 1833 she added an adjoining six or seven acre wood to the grounds. About the same time she also enlarged the house.

Anne extended the frontage of the house by the addition of another room at the northern end, which now forms part of the drawing room. She was probably also responsible at this time for the removal of the dividing wall which separated the other two front rooms, thus forming the present study. The "old" dining room and new kitchens were also added at the back of the house, extending it back towards the hillside as far as the archway. Perhaps in an attempt to "gentrify" the old cottage, in making her alterations she gave her new rooms greater height. Her dining room ceiling is a foot higher than the hall. The drawing room is also higher, resulting in unexpected changes in floor level in the corridors above. The original stables and coach house were probably also built now. All that remains of these old stables is now incorporated into the outbuildings of the Lodge.

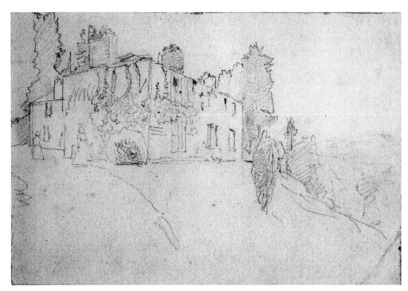

An anonymous sketch shows Ann Copley's extensions to the house

Anne Copley junior does not seem to have lived in the house permanently and in June 1841 she leased Brantwood for a year to James Clarke for £80, and from at least September 1843 she lived in York.

In York, the Copleys, the Hudsons and the Heslop families were all close friends. By March 1844 Anne Copley had leased Brantwood to

The Rev. Charles Hudson lived at Brantwood as a boy and was killed on the Matterhorn

Josiah Hudson and his family and they settled there; periodically the Heslops visited the Hudsons at Coniston, and the Hudsons often returned to York to see their friends.

Anne Copley died in York on 22 November 1845 leaving her property in the hands of her trustee, E.J. Copley. He tried unsuccessfully to sell Brantwood to the Rev. Thomas Mills for 2000 guineas. On 5 September 1846 Copley explained that the house was "occupied by my friend Mr Hudson and his family", and

9

in the next year he reduced the asking price to £1800. The attempted sale seems to have foundered in March 1849 when Copley said he would accept £1500 for it.

Meanwhile the Hudson family continued to live at Brantwood. Young Charles Hudson was about sixteen when the family moved to Coniston. He was educated at St Peter's, York, and in term time he lodged with the Heslops. Charles Hudson learned his love of mountains in the Lake District. On a walking holiday in Cumberland in 1845 he averaged twenty seven miles each day. By 1851 he was at St John's College, Cambridge, where he was a keen oarsman. He spent time climbing from Geneva in 1852-3 and on his return to England he became curate at St Mary's Church, Bridgnorth. In 1854 he served in the Crimea. He was an early member of the Alpine Club and in 1855 led a party of young Englishmen on a climb of Mont Blanc, without guides. He was killed on 14 July 1865 when he was a member of the first party to climb the Matterhorn.

In 1850 the Rev. John Heslop was staying with the Hudsons at Brantwood when he was taken ill, and died on 23 June.

An early reference to Brantwood appeared in *The Old Man, or Ravings and Ramblings around Conistone*, published in 1849, while the Hudsons were still living in the house:

> … The road runs between the lake and the most attractively placed villa of Brantwood, in the charming grounds of which is a seat called "Wordsworth's Seat" because that great poet is in the habit of recommending it to his friends as the point whence he thinks the beauties of Conistone are beheld to the most advantage …

The Hudsons must have left Brantwood early in 1852. In May of that year it became the home of William James Linton, artist, poet, political writer

William James Linton

Linton's press building on the south drive. The roof lights would have illuminated the type cases while the side windows provided light for the press.

and a foremost wood-engraver of his day. Brantwood's association with the literary and artistic world of Victorian England had begun. Linton moved to Brantwood from Miteside in Cumberland, renting the house in the first year from the Copley trustees, and finally raising a mortgage to buy it in March 1853 for £1000.

At the time of his removal to Brantwood he was the editor of a magazine called *The English Republic*. At Brantwood he set up his own printing press in the outbuildings which he erected for the purpose on the south drive, and with the help of a few friends printed the *Republic* and a similar magazine, *The Northern Tribune*.

One of Linton's helpers in the typographical venture, W. E. Adams, has explained that the press and type cases were originally installed in one of the bedrooms – probably the small room over the front door – until the

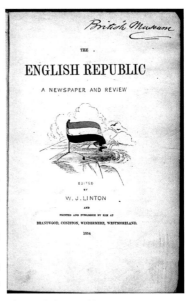

The English Republic, *Linton's Republican tract printed at Brantwood*

new building was ready to accommodate them. The outside walls of the building were adorned with *God and the People, Light more Light, Laborare est orare*, and other such revolutionary mottoes. A number of years ago flaking white-wash revealed one of these mottoes, painted in a fine large gothic script, on the north *inside* wall of the building.

Linton's other two printers were Thomas Hailing and George Vine. Two of them lodged at Yewdale Bridge, at the entrance to Coniston; the third had to walk as far as Torver.

Between 1852 and 1854 Linton was joined at Brantwood by his Polish friend Karl Stolzman and his wife. He came to help to teach Linton's three sons. Brantwood's ten bedrooms must have only just been sufficient at times. The press occupied one room (to start with); then there were frequent visitors, and, as W.E.Adams recorded:

The family at Brantwood in 1854 consisted of Mr and Mrs Linton and their six children – three boys and three girls – the youngest mere babies. The cleverest and most promising of the boys the second son, Lancelot – died early. All the children were charming romps, who made things lively for everybody about the place. Mrs Linton was an amiable lady – quiet, cheerful and contented – devoted to her children. The life at Brantwood was very secluded. Mr Linton busy with his engraving, his writing, and his correspondence, made few friends in the neighbourhood. I can recall only one, Dr Bywell, then in practice there – though once Harriet Martineau came over from Ambleside. Indeed, Mr Linton, as I know from my intercourse with the villagers in Coniston, was regarded as a considerable mystery, while the sort of work we were doing in the printing office caused us all to be viewed with suspicion.

Mr Linton had, however, a friend in Keswick, Dr Lietch, who had told him about a young lady there, a writer of novels and an ardent Radical, whose acquaintance he thought he ought to make. This of course, was Miss Lynn. Well, Miss Lynn was invited to Brantwood. She came for the first time while I was there. I remember her as a tall, stately, handsome young woman. We were all captivated by her appearance and manners. It was soon after this that Miss Lynn wrote for *The Republic* an article on Mary Woolstoncraft; also, I think, a notable poem in the same number signed

Popular novelist, Eliza Lynn Linton

'Agathon'. The good folks of Coniston, even before our impecunious days commenced, were disinclined to serve us. If we wanted to be clothed or shod, the tailor or the cordwainer, prior to taking our measure for suit or shoes, pointedly demanded, "When are ye gawin' to pay?" This want of faith in our honesty, as much as the suspicion of our proceedings, prevented any close communion between the natives and ourselves.

Linton's first wife died while they were at Brantwood and in 1857 he married Eliza Lynn who was already a popular writer, with three three-decker novels to her credit. In the following year the family moved to London but in

Linton's Claribel and other Poems *was published in 1865. He engraved this view from the study window as a vignette for the title page.*

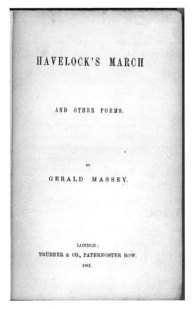

The title page of Massey's volume of poetry published in his Brantwood days.

1864, Linton who disliked town life, returned to Brantwood, his family joining him there for the summers. Several of Eliza Lynn's novels were written at Brantwood, including *Grasp your Nettle, Lizzie Lorton of Greyrigg*, and *Sowing the Wind*.

Linton explained in his *Memories* (1894) that he rented a garden and two fields between Brantwood and the lake, and had another small garden, "with bees, reached by steps to above the height of the house." He had the use of a horse, his cows grazed his two fields, he had a pig, poultry and pigeons. He also had some twenty sheep which grazed the fells above Brantwood. With the Fell Enclosure Acts, his sheep entitled him to an apportionment of six acres, increasing the Brantwood estate to sixteen acres.

13

We know from an Inventory of the contents of the house made in September 1867 that it was quite sparsely furnished. During his ownership his addition to the actual house comprised the building of the bow window in the study.

During the six years that the Lintons lived in London, Brantwood was let to the poet Gerald Massey. While he was living here his book, *Robert Burns, A Centenary Song, and other Lyrics* was published in 1859, and *Havelock's March and other Poems,* in 1861. In 1860 the dedication to an American edition of another volume of his poems was dated from Brantwood.

In 1867 Linton finally left Coniston to emigrate to America. In the few years immediately following his emigration, the house was rented during the summer months by the Rev. G.W. Kitchin, at that time Censor of Oxford non-collegiate students, and to become Dean of Winchester and later Durham. What happened to it during the remainder of the year is not clear. Linton's furniture remained in the house; perhaps some of his family lived there.

The central part of Ruskin's 1837 drawing of Coniston was engraved for his Poetry of Architecture. *The original drawing, in the Ruskin Museum, Coniston, reproduced here, clearly shows that he was in the harbour at Brantwood when he captured the view.*

2 *John Ruskin*

In its first seventy years Brantwood had sheltered many minor poets, authors and artists to give it some claim to fame, but in 1871 it was to become the home of one of the greatest of the Victorians.

John Ruskin, by this time a man of 52 and famous, had become a leading art critic and one of the most powerful influences on English art in the Victorian era soon after the publication of the first volume of his *Modern Painters* in 1843. Other books for which he is famous include *The Stones of Venice* (1851-3), *Unto this Last* (1860), *Sesame and Lilies* (1865), *Ethics of the Dust* and *Crown of Wild Olive* (1866), and perhaps most famous of all, his autobiography, *Praeterita* (1885-9). His best-seller is the fairy story *King of the Golden River*, first published in 1851. In 1869 Ruskin was elected the first Slade Professor of Fine Art at Oxford University. In 1871 he started to publish his periodical *Fors Clavigera* in which he aired his views on many subjects and in which he first proposed to establish his Utopian 'Guild of St George'.

In the summer of 1871, when recovering from a serious illness at Matlock in Derbyshire, Ruskin heard that Brantwood was for sale.

Ruskin made this sketch of Brantwood on his first visit to his new house on 12 September 1871. He sent it to Joan Severn to show her what Brantwood was like.

He did not know the house, but he knew its position and the view which it commanded. He had first visited Coniston as a small boy of five in 1824, and had long had an affection for the place. In 1837 he had actually landed from his rowing boat in Brantwood's harbour and drawn Coniston Hall across the lake, with the Old Man behind it. The harbour wall can be seen in his drawing.

While repairs were being carried out at Brantwood Ruskin took a group of friends to Italy. The group, photographed in Venice, comprised, from left to right, John Ruskin, Mrs Hilliard, Joan Severn, Arthur Severn, Constance Hilliard, Albert Goodwin.

Ruskin immediately offered to pay Linton his asking price of £1500 for the property. In September he went to visit his new home and found, as he wrote to various friends, "The view from the house is finer than I expected, the house itself dilapidated and rather dismal" (to his cousin Joan Severn); "On the whole, the finest view I know in Cumberland or Lancashire, the house – small, old, damp, and smoky-chimneyed" (to C.E.Norton); "It is a bit of steep hillside, facing west, ... The slope is half copse, half moor and rock – a pretty field beneath, less steep – a white two-storied cottage, and a bank of turf in front of it – then a narrow mountain road and on the other side of that – Naboth's vineyard – my neighbour's field, to the water's edge ..." (to Thomas Carlyle). To another correspondent Ruskin described the house as "a mere shed of rotten timber and loose stone".

But undeterred – he had been primarily interested in the view rather than the house – he made arrangements for the necessary repairs to be carried out. The repairs included having the roof of the original part of the house renewed. No doubt the elaborate barge boards at the southern end of the original building date from this time. Ruskin's first addition, made now, was the small turret room entered from his bedroom at the southern corner of the house. This turret has a magnificently wide view, north, south, and west, overlooking the lake, fells and mountains – in fact entirely capturing Father West's view.

Ruskin's first addition to the house, The Turret Room on the SW corner.

When he bought it, Ruskin described the house as "white". Recent scientific analysis of the external paintwork confirms what the American visitor, Elbert Hubbard wrote about "the old yellow house". Ruskin had the external walls painted yellow. He also had a special wallpaper made for the study and drawing room with its design based on the pattern on a damask sleeve in a National Gallery fifteenth century painting by Mario Marziale.

The repairs and additions were carried out by the local builders, but during Ruskin's absence in Italy, a superintending eye was kept on their activities by Ruskin's friend Thomas Richmond of Windermere, brother of the portrait painter, George Richmond.

The work was duly completed and Ruskin came to live in Brantwood for the first time on Friday, 12 September 1872. He brought with him his cousin, Joan Severn and her painter husband Arthur, son of Joseph Severn, the friend of Keats. She came to help with the arranging of the inside of the house. Brantwood was to become the Severns' second home for the next sixty years.

Ruskin's mother had died on 5 December 1871. He sold the family house at 163 Denmark Hill in south London, spending his last day there on 28 March 1872. The furniture which he wished to retain was

The Lodge. The Victoria in the photograph was probably bought by the Severns in the 1880s.

sent either to Brantwood, or to his rooms at Corpus Christi College, Oxford, where he wrote in his diary on 29 March, "In my college rooms, having finally left my old home".

Brantwood was not left long without builders. Towards the end of 1872 work began at the end of the south drive. The old stable block (shown in the plan on the Linton-Ruskin conveyance to be a little larger than Brantwood itself) was almost completely demolished. On its site, Ruskin built a new lodge for his valet Frederick Crawley. It was finished in the following spring. Ruskin planned the lodge with much care and again one finds angle windows to capture the views. When finished,

Joan Severn seated against the southern wall of the new dining room about 1915.

the new building was nearly as large as Brantwood, but, being essentially an impractical man, Ruskin omitted to include a front door in his design. He decided to have a vine growing on the front wall instead!

In September 1878 Ruskin was planning to build a small block onto the southern wall of the house. This would have provided him with a fireproof room for his

Ruskin's silhouette sketch of himself leading a working party to a steep part of the estate, probably on 15 September 1881

extensive collection of Turner watercolours, leading off his study, with a small dressing room above, entered from his bedroom.

Arthur Severn's painting of the path to the gate of The Professor's Garden.

19

However, events overtook this scheme. Towards the end of November he gave up his rooms in Oxford, with the result that all of the furniture, pictures and books which he had there, had to be moved to Brantwood – where there was insufficient space. The answer was to build a new, single-storey dining room onto the southern end of the house. This room, with its magnificent views across and down the lake, and its French window, has seven lancet windows in its south wall, said by some to represent *The Seven Lamps of Architecture*. A photograph of a group of people standing on the frozen lake, which must have been taken in January 1879, shows the completed dining room in the background. This released the old dining room, a dark, viewless room off the hall as one enters the front door, to become a secondary library.

Ruskin delighted in walking and working on his small estate. He had brought his head gardener, David Downs, with him from London, and visitors to the house were often pressed into service in various projects. Two Oxford students staying at Brantwood in the summer of 1875 to help with the translation of Xenophon's *Economist* helped with the digging and enlargement of the harbour. Paths and steps were cut,

A group on the frozen lake in January 1879. Ruskin stands with his alpenstock, his valet Baxter to the right. The lady on the left of the group is probably Mrs Fanny Talbot, an early benefactress of the Guild of St George and the National Trust. The recently finished dining room can be seen above.

Beehive shelter in The Professor's Garden.

bridges built over small streams. In the woods behind the house Ruskin created his own cottage garden, with espalier apple trees, gooseberry bushes, strawberries and flowers. In one corner were beehives, while the other side of the Professor's Garden is flanked by a steep watercourse.

Across the tumbling stream which forms the southern boundary of the Professor's Garden is a stone seat built for Ruskin to sit and watch the rushing water. Wandering in Susan Beever's garden across the lake at The Thwaite in 1884 Ruskin had seen and admired her "two deeply interesting thrones of the ancient Abbots of Furness". She sent her gardener to Brantwood to build one for Ruskin.

Ruskin's stone seat from where …

… he watched the tumbling beck.

21

Dating from Ruskin's early days at Brantwood is a zig-zag path rising up the steep hillside from what is now the car park. On this path were constructed a series of small terraces to support more gardening experiments. Writing to Joan Severn about his ideas for this part of the garden, he explained that the zig-zag path was to be an allegorical approach to his paradise terraces, inspired by Dante's *Divine Comedy*.

Work was progressing on the formation of a fish pond in 1877-8, and in June 1879 guests and gardeners were grubbing out roots, just beyond the stone seat, to form a tennis court. Enthusiastic but impractical Ruskin had made the task more difficult by cutting down the trees here, thus his helpers had no leverage "to pull the roots up with". Towards the end of 1881 Ruskin turned his attention higher still on the hillside behind the

Laurence Hilliard's sketch of Ruskin pausing during a tree-cutting afternoon, perhaps 23 July 1876.

W.G. Collingwood's view of Coniston seen over one of the reservoir sluices.

The Coach House, with the stables behind. The coachman lived over the Coach House while the loft above the stables was for fodder and storage.

house. Here he created his Moorland Garden. On 25 October he told Joan Severn that he had two of the local builder's men and other helpers "all in full force on the bit of ground and it is really coming into form fast". Part of it was boggy and the water drained into a small stream. Two reservoirs were dug in the bed of the stream; eventually the local builders had to be called in to make them watertight and to build sluice gates; the blacksmith created decorative handles so that the sluices could be opened to allow the water to rush downhill and form a waterfall – at will – opposite the front door. Into the hillside nearby Ruskin built an equally unsuccessful ice house.

If Ruskin wanted a carriage he hired one from Mrs Sly at the Waterhead Hotel. Then in 1881-2, probably largely for the Severns, Ruskin built the present coach house with stables – stalls and loose boxes – behind. This was a considerable undertaking. As Ruskin reported to Joan Severn, the blasting blew about a hundred tons of white clay loose and that had to be carted away "before we can ask what next!" Below, the land now occupied by the car park, was developed as a kitchen garden. Ruskin

The six cypress trees flanking what is now the south east corner of the car park.

23

John Ruskin, Joan Severn and a group of friends in front of the drawing room windows.
A previously unpublished photograph by T. A. & J. Green of Grasmere taken in September
1881.

disapproved of glasshouses but eventually he had one built for Mrs
Severn towards the northern end of this garden, below the stables.
Across the road, near the path leading to the lake, is an orchard. Ruskin
traditionally brought six "cypress" trees back from Italy and planted
them in the orchard and kitchen garden. In the 1890s they were moved
into a line on the southern flank of the large kitchen garden where they
grew into a well-known feature of the landscape, surviving until the
1980s. Also in the 1890s the great rhododendron bank near the car park
was brought here from Collingwood's garden at Lanehead.

As Ruskin grew older, and his health deteriorated in the 1890s, he
was less able to look after the gardens and paths that he had created and
they fell into disuse and became overgrown. Increasingly Joan Severn
moulded the grounds to her own taste. The High Walk, running south
from the old tennis court, was planted with exotic trees and rare shrubs;
azaleas and rhododendrons abound. Probably also about now more

Joan Severn photographed near one of her new greenhouses in the kitchen garden.

greenhouses were added at the northern end of the kitchen garden. A vine was planted in one of them.

Ruskin had brought David Downs, his head gardener, with him from London in the 1870s, and he would have dealt with much of the early development of the grounds at Brantwood. Eventually he left Brantwood in the late 1870s to live at and manage the Guild of St George's farm at Totley, Sheffield. He was succeeded as head gardener and general factotum by Dawson Herdson, who must have worked at Brantwood since 1871. Across the road from the kitchen garden and glass houses the path to the lake was improved by the construction of the Harbour Walk. Joan Severn and Dawson Herdson worked on this together, planting more azaleas and lilacs. The work was completed on the day Herdson retired in 1898 or 1899.

Meanwhile throughout the eighties the house was continually being enlarged for the benefit of the Severns and their

The azalea-lined Harbour Walk

Brantwood gradually grew up the hillside. The original cottage can be identified behind the new dining room. The turret window at the front corner of the second floor is in The School Room. The Studio is at the right of the house, seen behind the Linton building.

five children. By 1885 a second floor had been added to the bulk of the house, to provide the School Room and five more bedrooms. At the same time the roof above the original kitchen wing was raised and a new window was built into its western wall, to provide a large storage room entered from the new School Room. Extending this second floor still further, a large Studio was built, probably in 1886, onto the back of the

Arthur Severn's Studio. His 1898-9 portrait of Ruskin hangs on the end wall. The articulated model of a bird's wing was made to illustrate one of Ruskin's Love's Meine lectures in 1873.

26

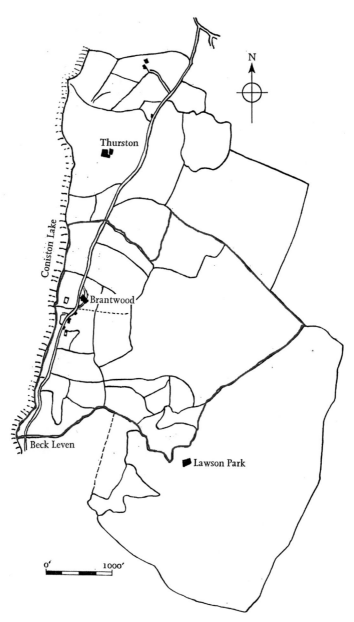

Map of the Brantwood estate in 1931. The estate today is outlined in red.

house for Arthur Severn. This was built partly onto the hillside itself, and has its own outside door. The Studio was equipped with its own central heating system, and an acetylene lighting plant was housed in a wooden building at the back, to serve two elaborate bracket lamps on either side of the fireplace alcove.

The 1905 extension to the drawing room, with balcony above and heptangular rooms beyond.

Because of his deteriorating health, in 1885 Ruskin executed a Deed of Gift in which he made over Brantwood and its contents to the Severns, although of course the property remained nominally his during his lifetime.

In the next decade, several purchases of land by Mrs Severn (no doubt using Ruskin's money) increased the size of the estate to almost 500 acres. In his own name, Ruskin never owned any more than the sixteen acres he had bought from Linton. The additions to the estate included the house Thurston, then called Coniston Bank, Low Bank Ground, and on the fells, the Lawson Park Farm, established in the 14th century as a sheep farm by the monks of Furness Abbey. Also included

Arthur Severn's watercolour of the rose arches edging the new terrace outside the drawing room windows.

Lily Severn's sitting room in the Lodge. The wall hanging covers the internal door.

in the estate was the small Fir Island in the lake, now the property of the National Trust. Along the road, the estate stretched for about a mile and a quarter, almost from Lanehead to Beck Leven, although the total north-south length of the estate was nearer to a mile and a half.

On 20 January 1900 John Ruskin died. The house and contents were inherited by Joan and Arthur Severn. They further enlarged the house in 1905 by the addition of the bay window to the drawing room and the heptangular sitting room which leads from it; above, it provided Arthur with a dressing room leading off Joan's bedroom which now had a balcony.

Lack of space was a constant problem for the Severns. Brantwood must have been much too small for them. The 1901 Census shows that on 31 March, Joan Severn, sons "young"

Lily Severn and her brothers with the sitting room's external staircase.

Arthur and Herbert, and daughter Lily were at home. Agnew would have been away at Oxford, and presumably Arthur and his daughter Violet were in London. John Wilson, the coachman, probably lived in the room above the front of the coach house. Ruskin's former valet, Peter Baxter and his wife and one of their daughters lived in the Lodge, but in addition to that, Lily Severn occupied one of the Lodge's bedrooms as a sitting room. Also living in Brantwood were the cook and five maids.

The Severns continued to divide their time between Coniston and London where the lease of their house at 28 Herne Hill, given to them as a wedding present by Ruskin in 1871, expired in 1907. They then leased a more fashionable

A page from Ruskin's St Louis Psalter, *c.1260. Perhaps his most treasured medieval manuscript, it was sold by the Severns in 1904. Its price would have paid for the 1905 extensions and kept the Severns in comfort for some time.*

house at 9 Warwick Square, Victoria. When they moved between Coniston and London, the staff and the silver left on the first train, the Severns following later in the day enabling the house to be opened up in time for dinner. Meanwhile, at Coniston the Baxters moved into Brantwood for the duration of the sojourn in London. There was one member of staff permanently resident at Warwick Square.

Their five children, Arthur, Agnew and Herbert, Lily and Violet, must have been nearly as expensive to maintain as Brantwood itself. To augment their inadequate income the Severns gradually sold off the principal treasures of the house – the medieval manuscripts, many of museum quality, the bulk of the Turner watercolours, the Italian sculptures, the Scott manuscripts.

Pre-Raphalite painter William Holman Hunt photograhed with Ruskin at Brantwood in September 1894.

In his will, dated 23 October 1883, Ruskin showed the affection he had for his home at Coniston. Bequeathing his estate to the Severns he "earnestly prayed" them to maintain the estate in "decent order" and "to accord during thirty consecutive days in every year such permission to strangers to see the house and pictures as I have done in my lifetime." After Ruskin's death the Severns were quick to forget his testamentary wishes. A local guide book of the time tells visitors that the house is neither a museum nor is it open to the public.

The new tennis court in the field in front of the house may also have been paid for by the sale of the St Louis Psalter. Arthur Severn photographed with members of his family.

31

Joan preferred Brantwood to London life and she died here in 1924. Lily, her elder daughter, has already died in 1920. Thereafter, Arthur who preferred London to Coniston, spent most of his life in the south, usually only returning to Brantwood to search for something else to sell. Young Arthur had been established with a Fish Hatchery at Bibury and took no interest in Brantwood. Agnew married, had no children and died in 1929. Herbert became an engineer, living, I think, in Barrow, leaving the younger daughter, Violet, in solitary splendour at Brantwood.

Arthur Severn died in London in 1931. The Trustees had already begun to disperse the remaining contents of the house, with a sale at Sotheby's on 24 July 1930 of *The Manuscripts and Remaining Library of John Ruskin.*

The glory that was Brantwood had passed. Among well-known visitors to the house in the period 1871-1931 had been Lady Burne-Jones, W. Holman Hunt, Sir Henry Acland, Harvey Goodwin, Bishop of Carlisle, A.W. Hunt, Coventry Patmore, Charles Darwin, sculptors Benjamin Creswick, Conrad Dressler and Gutzon Borglum, J.A.Froude, publisher George Allen, novelist Marie Correlli, artists Walter Crane, Albert Goodwin and Kate Greenaway, Sir Sydney Cockerell, Benjamin Jowett, Master of Balliol College, Oxford – and a host of others.

The remnants of Brantwood's fine collections were dispersed in a series of sales at Sotheby's in 1931, and finally in an incredibly ill-managed three day sale on the premises at the end of July 1931. Violet Severn continued to live in the house until June 1932 with the pieces of furniture she had retained for her new home in Coniston. She was cared for by the Wilkinson family who continued to live in the Lodge until the 1960s.

Laurence Hilliard painted the waterfall opposite the front door in 1885. The ice house is in the trees to the left of the steps.

3 The house in Ruskin's time

Since Brantwood is shown to members of the public primarily because it was Ruskin's home, a brief description of the house as it was in his lifetime may be of interest.

As the visitor to the house waited at the front door (not the door by which present visitors enter), he would notice outside a curious array of slate blocks on a wooden frame. This was Ruskin's "rock harmonicon", a set of musical stones which is still to be seen in the Coniston Museum. Behind him, a small waterfall would come tumbling down off the fells, controlled by the reservoirs on the hillside above.

The front door. The wooden pillars have been given new bases since Ruskin's time.

The hall is one of the four ground floor rooms of the original cottage and when Ruskin bought Brantwood it had the largest uninterrupted wall-space in the house. The doorway in the facing wall has been

opened up from a wall cupboard on the kitchen side since Ruskin's time. Nevertheless this wall was too small and also unsuitable for Ruskin's two large Turner paintings – *The Slave Ship*, which he sold to America, for a little over 2000 guineas (it is now in the Museum of Fine Arts in Boston) and *The Grand Canal, Venice*, which he sold soon afterwards for £4000 (now, Henry E. Huntington Library and Art Gallery in California).

Turner's painting of The Grand Canal, Venice, *five feet high (excluding its frame), was too large to hang at Brantwood.*

This early view of Brantwood by Arthur Severn shows the old dining room, to the left, at the back of the house.

In the centre of the hall was a circular rosewood table used for bedroom candlesticks, and to one side was a mahogany side table with a marble top. By the side of the front door was a small fireplace, and round the corner near the foot of the stairs, the green baize door led to the kitchens. There were drawings by Burne-Jones and Ruskin himself on the walls. Two small mahogany hall chairs are still in the house.

To the left was the old dining room. Here were portraits by Northcote of Ruskin's parents, two *Annunciations* by Tintoretto, and the youthful Turner's self-portrait. After the new dining room was built, this room was re-arranged to become a secondary library containing many books, and drawer after drawer of Ruskin's own sketches, letters and manuscripts. Two of the bookcases then in this room are now in the study. Concealed behind or under one of them was found in 1931 a group of letters from Ruskin to Effie Gray, and a copy of his *Sesame and Lilies* inscribed to Rose La Touche possibly put there to keep them from the eyes of the editors of the Ruskin *Library Edition*. Probably after Ruskin's time the far end of this room was partitioned off to form a small cloak room.

Ruskin's Rock Harmonicon is now in the Coniston Museum

34

The drawing room, overlooking the lake, was only three-quarters of its present size in Ruskin's time. The bay window and the heptangular room leading from it were added early in 1905. This room was overcrowded in a typically Victorian fashion. The wallpaper here, as in the study, had been specially made but little of it could be seen because bookcases and pictures occupied almost all of the wall space. The piano stood near the window and behind

The drawing room alcove with the shelf cabinet and Ruskin's St Mark's.

One of Ruskin's finest architectural studies, the N.W. Porch of St. Mark's sometimes hung over the Shell cabinet.

it, flanked by two bookcases, stood his mother's secretaire (still in its original position). At the other end of the room, in the arched alcove, was a cabinet containing Ruskin's collection of shells.

Ruskin frequently re-hung the pictures on his walls. When he first moved to Brantwood he had watercolours by Hunt over the shell cabinet. Later he replaced them with three Prouts. Subsequently he changed this wall again to hold Turner's *Constance*, two of his own studies of Abbeville and six Prouts. These were flanked by Burne-Jones's *Fair Rosamund* and *A Country Girl* attributed to Gainsborough which was subsequently moved nearer to the window. Later, his own fine study of *The North West Porch of St Mark's, Venice*, took pride of place above the shell cabinet with his own copy of *Zipporah* after Botticelli to its right. It was in this room where breakfast was taken daily – strawberries and cream at 10 – while Ruskin read aloud the results of his morning's writing.

Ruskin's 1874 study of Zipporah, *one of the daughters of Jethro, after Botticelli, hangs to the right of the shelf cabinet.*

But it was the study which was the real heart and treasure house of Brantwood, two of the ground floor rooms of the original cottage had been made one before Linton's time. He made the small bow window in which stood the octagonal table at which Ruskin wrote in the winter. This was the "Winter Table". His arm chair and fire screens still stand nearby. Fitted open bookshelves were on either side of the fireplace – reference books on the left, history on the right. Turner's *Lake of Geneva* hung originally over the fireplace, brought here from a comparable position in the study of the Denmark Hill house. It was replaced about 1881 by Luca della Robbia's *Madonna and Child* and more shelves to hold specimens of ancient pottery and other antiquities. The pieces from Cyprus came as a result of Ruskin's sponsorship of General Cesnola's excavations. Those from Corfu, Patmos and Athens were bought from the Adams Collection on Ruskin's behalf by C.E.Norton.

On the wall facing the bay window were six more Turner watercolours: *Farnley, Terni, Arona, Bonneville, Narni* and *Splügen*. Further along the same wall, on the other side of the door, was a large bookcase, glazed above and cupboarded below, which had come from Denmark Hill. Adjacent to it and facing the fireplace were the mineral cabinets – three of them spaced to fill the south wall, and with a bookcase, probably specially made to fit across their tops in this location. In the cabinet drawers was part of the important Stowe collection of minerals bought by

Fair Rosamund *by Sir Edward Burne-Jones. This was bought by Ruskin's father in 1863.*

Ruskin from the Duke of Buckingham. In front of the cabinets was the "Summer Desk" at which Ruskin worked in the summer months – and in front of that, standing in the middle of the room (as it still does) was another cabinet containing framed drawings by himself, Bewick, Hunt and others; next to it stood a Turner cabinet. Near to this cabinet and between the two windows were the "Natural History" and "Botany" bookcases. Among the other treasures in the study were the original manuscripts of several of Sir Walter Scott's novels, *Peveril of the Peak, The Black Dwarf,* and *The Fortunes of Nigel,* a substantial collection of medieval manuscripts, and of course the manuscripts of many of his own books.

The winter table stands by the study bow window near the fire-place. Opposite the window Turner watercolours almost cover the specially-made wallpaper.

The new dining room, built in 1878-9, is one of the largest and lightest rooms in the house. Facing the visitor as he entered the room was the portrait of Ruskin as "The author of *Modern Painters*" by

George Richmond. On a sideboard below it stood, to the left, a white marble statue of Nike standing on a globe, which came from a Temple of Neptune on Corfu. This was once in Ruskin's rooms at Oxford. It dates from the late Hellenistic period and is now in Newcastle University's

Emily Warren's watercolour of the southern end of the study, The Summer Desk. *Many of Ruskin's medieval manuscripts were kept in the bookcase above the mineral cabinets; the snow-capped Old Man can be seen through the window.*

Greek Museum. On the other end of this sideboard stood a 13th-14th century marble statue of a pelican feeding her young. This was probably the work of Giovanni Pisano, and was given to Ruskin by Francesca Alexander when he met her in Florence in 1882.

To the left, on the end wall above another sideboard, hung the three family portraits by James Northcote. The three and a half years old John Ruskin, with the famous "boo hills" as his background, hung in the centre, flanked on either side by his parents. So many of the treasures in this room were of museum quality. The "boo hills" portrait was bought several years ago by the National Portrait Gallery so that it could be re-hung at Brantwood. Supported on brackets on either side of this painting were two marble pilasters with the angels of the Apocalypse, probably also by Pisano, and bought from Brantwood between 1904 and 1911 by the Metropolitan Museum of Art in New York. To the left of Margaret Ruskin, behind the door, was a third marble Pisano pilaster with the symbols of SS. Matthew, Mark and Luke. This has also found its way to the same American museum.

On the long wall, above the fireplace hung a portrait of the Venetian Doge Andrea Gritti. Ruskin thought it was by Titian, but it is now attributed to Catena. The Severns had Collingwood paint a copy of it before they sold the original to the National Gallery about 1918. The "Titian" was produced as evidence at the Whistler v. Ruskin libel action to illustrate what Ruskin considered to be "sound workmanship".

Also on this wall was a portrait by Raphael, an early self-portrait of J.M.W.Turner, c.1793, now in the Indianapolis Museum of Art, and another portrait of John James Ruskin. This portrait was painted in 1802 by George Watson

The statue of Nike was obtained for Ruskin by Charles Eliot Norton.

The sideboard end of the dining room with the family portraits. The Nike *and the* Pelican *stand on the other sideboard to the right.*

This Pisano sculpture of Two Angels of the Apocalypse *was to the left of Northcote's portrait of the infant Ruskin.*

when the sitter was seventeen years old and about to move from Edinburgh to London to make his fortune. The artist became the first president of the Royal Scottish Academy, 1826-37; both he and his subject had taken lessons from Alexander Nasmyth in Edinburgh – perhaps indeed they were friends.

The staircase walls were decorated by some of Turner's sepia drawings, and there was a photograph of Philip Burne-Jones's portrait of his father. The first room at the top, the Turret Room, was Ruskin's bedroom until 1878 when an illness and a series of unpleasant dreams drove him next door. This is a small room, but again the walls were lined with some of Turner's most highly finished watercolours – twenty of them – with a still life of fruit by W.H.Hunt above the mantlepiece, "hanging among the Turners

The dining room fireplace wall, with Catena's Doge Andrea Gritti *over the fireplace and the Watson portrait of* John James Ruskin *on the left of this wall. The dining table must have had several of its leaves removed.*

like a brooch", and his father's watercolour of *Conway Castle*. Among the Turners were views of *Goldau, Constance, Flint, Coblentz, Gosport,* and *Richmond, Surrey* – the Ruskins' first Turner purchase. When, in 1993, the Turners in this room were valued for me, the then total was an amazing £6,340,000.

The view from The Turret Room.

41

Ruskin's bedroom with its Turner-covered walls

Towards the end of his life, when he found the narrow staircase difficult, Ruskin used the Turret Room as a sitting room, and it was here in 1899 that J.Howard Whitehouse presented to him a National Address of Congratulation on his eightieth birthday.

John James Ruskin's Conway Castle *hangs above the fireplace.*

Of the other bedrooms, Arthur Severn's room was the small one on the right at the top of the stairs, but he seems to have occupied the Turret Room on its vacation by Ruskin. Joan Severn had the large room over the drawing room, while their daughter Violet used the room over the front door. (It seems

Still life of fruit by W. H. Hunt hangs below Conway Castle.

likely that this had originally been Linton's press room.) On the second floor, the room with the large window overlooking the dining room was the Severn children's School-Room. The three boys had their rooms on this floor.

J. Howard Whitehouse, photographed by the author at Bembridge in summer 1947.

43

4 *The Ruskin Memorial*

In Birmingham John Howard Whitehouse probably left school at the age of fourteen and continued his education at night classes at Midland College. Here, Howard S. Pearson introduced him to Ruskin's teaching. In 1896 Whitehouse was a founder member of the new Birmingham Ruskin Society. It was with the secretary of the Liverpool Ruskin Society that Whitehouse visited Ruskin at Brantwood on his eightieth birthday. Eleven months later he was at Coniston again for Ruskin's funeral. He became secretary at the Ruskin-inspired Toynbee Hall when William Beveridge (the author of our Welfare State) and T. Edmund Harvey (later M.P. for the Combined Universities) were Sub-Warden and Deputy Warden. Harvey and Whitehouse became Companions of Ruskin's Guild of St George, Harvey following in Ruskin's footsteps as Master from 1934 to 1950 with Whitehouse as Trustee from 1918 until his death in 1955.

W. G. Collingwood's painting of Ruskin's boat Jumping Jenny *off Brantwood about 1885*

Following a successful parliamentary career, in 1919 Whitehouse founded Bembridge School in the Isle of Wight, to successfully test some of Ruskin's, and some of his own, educational theories. He collected Ruskin material throughout his life and built galleries at Bembridge to house his collection. In 1925 he visited Arthur Severn at Brantwood where he stayed for a few days, trying to buy Brantwood on behalf of the Guild "as a place of pilgrimage for ever in honour of The Master". After two or three years the negotiations foundered.

By the time of Severn's death in 1931 his daughter

Arthur Severn's sketch of Ruskin's secretary Laurence Hilliard in 1883; he designed the Jumping Jenny *in 1879. Hilliard died in 1887.*

Violet was leading a Miss Havisham-like existence at Brantwood with bowls and buckets strategically placed in rooms to collect dripping rain water. At the 1930-31 dispersal sales Whitehouse was a principal buyer. In 1932 the house and estate were offered for sale in eight lots, without attracting much interest. Ultimately Whitehouse bought four lots, giving him the house and outbuildings and 250 acres of surrounding land, for which he paid £7000. Ruskin had paid £1500 for a very much smaller house and sixteen acres of land sixty years earlier.

With the house, Whitehouse acquired, probably as gifts from Violet Severn, the dining table and most of the dining chairs, Ruskin's carriage and his boat, the *Jumping Jenny*. Some other furniture was bought and in April 1934 Brantwood was opened to the public. Whitehouse subsequently wrote "The house threatened speedily to become a ruin. Of all the opportunities which have been mine, I look back upon none with more satisfaction and pleasure than being able to acquire the home of John Ruskin and secure it for the nation."

Mr & Mrs Kenneth Romney-Townrow were established as resident hosts, looking after people who wished to stay at Brantwood, and conducting visitors around the house. Their pet deer hound is buried in the grounds, with its inscribed gravestone. Another early host was Arthur Windsor Richards who took a great interest in the wild life of the estate and wrote a number of charming books based on his observations there.

Ruskin's first bedroom. The Turret Room, today. Here is his bed; Hunt's Fruit *and J. J. Ruskin's* Conway Castle *hang over the fireplace surrounded by reproductions of his Turners.*

During the war Bembridge School was evacuated to the Waterhead Hotel in Coniston, and to Lake Villas, bought after the death of Violet Severn. Whitehouse's valuable Ruskin collection was moved from Bembridge and stored at Brantwood, which was also occasionally used by the school.

In 1944, in order to preserve its continuity as a Ruskin Memorial, Whitehouse presented the house and estate to Oxford University. However, in 1947, for various reasons, the university found itself unable to retain the gift and in due course it was returned to Whitehouse. He immediately transferred it to his own foundation, Education Trust Ltd, in whose ownership it remains.

After Whitehouse's death in 1955 the property came under the immediate care of his successor as chairman of Education Trust, Mr R.G. Lloyd (late Lord Lloyd of Kilgerran). Lord and Lady Lloyd, and now their family, spared no expense or effort to ensure that the house continues to be run as Whitehouse wished – as a memorial to Ruskin and as a study centre for adult education.

Parts of the house have always been open to the public, except during the war years. In the 1950s other parts of the house were used as a residential study centre by the Council for Nature and Twickenham College of Technology. At one time it came under the wing of Manchester University. Eventually an increase in leisure and tourism, coupled with generous help from various sponsors has made it possible to have almost the whole house open and to restore the estate to what it was in Ruskin's and the Severns' time. More and more furniture and other treasures have been restored to the house, and it now may be seen very much as it was when John Ruskin lived here.

The Lord Lloyd of Kilgerran opening the author's History of Brantwood *exhibition in The Coach House Gallery on 9 August 1975.*

The dining room today, with Northcote's portrait of Ruskin above his sideboard, looking down on his dining table and chairs.

47

W. G. Collingwood's painting of Brantwood from the lake as it was at the time of Ruskin's death in 1900.

A summer view of Brantwood with the lake and Coniston beyond, today.

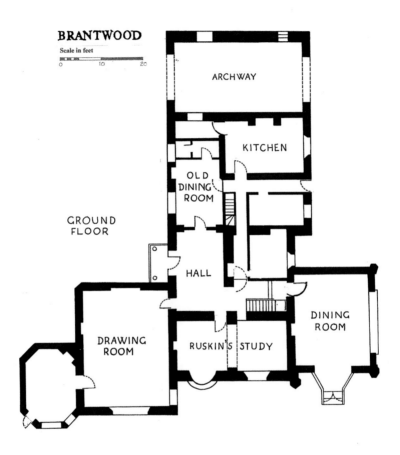

BRANTWOOD

Scale in feet

0   10   20

ARCHWAY

KITCHEN

OLD
DINING
ROOM

GROUND
FLOOR

HALL

DRAWING
ROOM

RUSKIN'S STUDY

DINING
ROOM

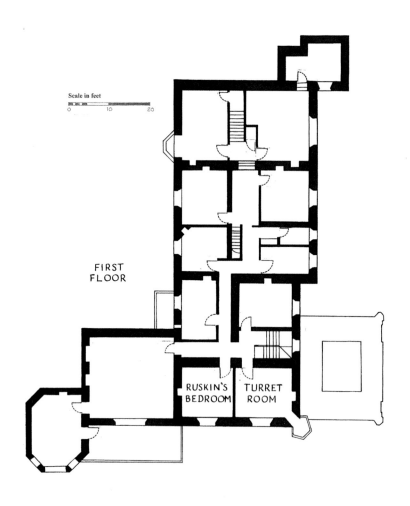

Scale in feet

0   10   20

FIRST
FLOOR

RUSKIN'S
BEDROOM

TURRET
ROOM

50

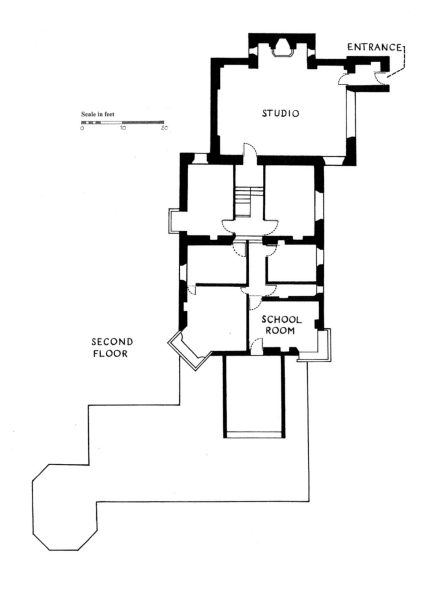

ENTRANCE

STUDIO

Scale in feet

0   10   20

SECOND
FLOOR

SCHOOL
ROOM

51